T0387944

Nevertheless

Never

theless

A Choreographic Workbook

Yvonne Rainer *with*
Emmanuèle Phuon

Illustrations by
Pascal Lemaître

Yale University Press
New Haven and London

Published with assistance from the foundation established in memory of Amasa Stone Mather of the Class of 1907, Yale College.

Yale University Press books may be purchased in quantity for educational, business, or promotional use. For information, please e-mail sales.press@yale.edu (U.S. office) or sales@yaleup.co.uk (U.K. office).

Designed by Dustin Kilgore.
Set in ITC American Typewriter type by Motto Publishing Services.
Printed in the United States of America.

Library of Congress Control Number: 2024946035
ISBN 978-0-300-27928-3 (hardcover : alk. paper)

A catalogue record for this book is available from the British Library.
This paper meets the requirements of ANSI/NISO Z39.48-1992 (Permanence of Paper).
10 9 8 7 6 5 4 3 2 1

Contents

Introduction
Emmanuèle Phuon

In 1999, Mikhail Baryshnikov invited Yvonne Rainer to make a new piece for his White Oak Dance Project. At the time, I was one of the dancers in his company, and I am ashamed to admit that I had never heard of her, or of the Judson Dance Theater, which she helped found. In my defense, I lived in Cambodia and Thailand until age sixteen. Also, Rainer had been absent from the dance world for the previous twenty-five years, pursuing a career as a filmmaker. The piece she choreographed for White Oak, *After Many a Summer Dies the Swan* (1999), marked her return to dance and, as I like to say, the beginning of our relationship. (Though we can find an earlier connection between us, as Rainer staged two anti–Vietnam War protests, *M-Walk* and *Trio A with Flags* in 1970, engaging with the same war that turned my life upside down.) After White Oak, I joined her informal company as one of the "Raindears,"[1] as she affectionately calls her group of dancers, and had the immense honor of participating in her creative process for five evening-length dance works.

What I did not know then was that Yvonne Rainer and her peers—among them, Steve Paxton, Trisha Brown, Lucinda Childs, and David Gordon—were part of the Judson Dance Theater, a collective of dancers, composers, and visual artists who laid the foundation for how we make and see dance today. Informed by the avant-garde in the visual arts and music—people such as the composer John

1. The original Raindears were Pat Catterson, Patricia Hoffbauer, Sally Silvers, and Emily Coates. Keith Sabado and I joined the group in 2009 and 2010, respectively, followed by David Thomson a few years later. Newer arrivals include Brittany Bailey and Elliot Mercer.

Cage and painter Robert Rauschenberg, who were themselves inspired by the French painter Marcel Duchamp—the Judson artists questioned the nature of dance performance: its aesthetics, codification, and traditional concert format. They danced in gymnasiums, lofts, parks, and streets, reconfiguring the relationship between audience and performers in terms of space and dynamics. Focused on the process over the finished performance, they introduced chance procedures and improvisation to their artwork, following the lead of John Cage's musical experiments. From Duchamp's ideas about art and the example of his Readymades—"found" objects that the artist exhibited as works of art—they built a new movement vocabulary out of the pedestrian activities of everyday life.

This strategy opened the field to anybody (and any body type) who wanted to dance, not just specialists. Rejecting storytelling, grand themes, and the monumental, the Judson artists resorted to game structures, collages, and task-based activities, turning the quotidian into art. They collaborated across disciplines, creating multi-disciplinary works. The 1960s offered fertile ground for artists in the United States, and many of these experimental ideas also arose from the geopolitical context of the sixties: the Vietnam War, and the pro-individual and collective freedom movements for civil rights, feminism, gay rights, and the environment, among others. Yvonne Rainer, one of the leaders of Judson Dance, the person who first coined the term *postmodern* to describe the work they were doing, is a dance legend.

The experience of working with Yvonne for the past fifteen years continues to nourish my work as a dancer and a choreographer. Thanks to Yvonne,

I have learned that humor is essential—both while making the dance and in its final performance. In the film *Marcel Duchamp: A Game of Chess,* we hear Duchamp say, "One of the things that interested me was introducing humor into my productions. It wasn't just humor for laughs, it wasn't black humor either. It was really a humor that added something . . . serious, if I dare say so."[2] That's the kind of humor I am talking about—serious humor, the kind that makes you think and question because it makes you see things from an unexpected angle. I learned that translating ideas into a dance or an image requires a lot of research to gain familiarity and intimacy with your topic of choice. That trusting my collaborators—dancers, dramaturgs, designers—always enriched the work beyond my expectations and capabilities. Finally, like many choreographers, I find myself deconstructing movement sequences and narratives, juxtaposing disparate theatrical elements to create additional layers of meaning, using text-based sequences, found material, pedestrian actions, and tasks. These strategies and ideas have become so prevalent today that we forget that they stem from the intense and radical period when Yvonne Rainer and her contemporaries challenged the very definition of dance.

Yvonne shared the material in this book when an injury prevented me from demonstrating or participating physically in class. I knew as soon as I held the pages in my hand that we should publish them. I also knew exactly how we should do it.

2. Jean-Marie Drot, director. *Jeu d'échecs avec Marcel Duchamp,* ORTF, 1963. Copyright © Succession Marcel Duchamp, 2016.

This book highlights her pedagogy, but it does not aim to be pedagogical. Rather, it is an invitation to join the creative process, offering a glimpse into her particular brand of whimsy—the quality that makes her dances so poetic and thoughtful.

In the first part of the book, "Nevertheless," Rainer deconstructs the body into separate parts to analyze how each unit moves. This text dates to a workshop she taught in her loft in SoHo toward the end of the sixties. She recorded it on a cassette tape to play it in a loop, letting the students interact with the instructions as they saw fit. This strategy allowed her to join the class with them, thus erasing all hierarchical relationships and avoiding interference with their discovery process. Once she even napped in the corner of the room. In the same spirit, readers can use this section of the book as a guide to research: they can aim to discover the body anew and break away from habitual pathways by reconsidering ab initio the role of each articulation, limb, and muscle group, and how they relate to one another. Increasingly adventurous movers may choose to change the order of the text to recombine paragraphs/body parts in an infinity of variations. They may choose to ignore the instructions or purposefully go against the text in a playful dialogue of voice and movement. (They should keep in mind, however, that although they can go against the text from time to time, it is more helpful to have something in which to ground the improvisation than to start with the idea that they will go against it.) In the process, to quote from André Breton when he discovered Lautréamont's *The Songs of Maldoror,* they will look for moments "as beautiful as the chance encounter of a sewing machine and an umbrella on an operating table." Fortuitous relationships between action and text, new pathways, situations, and gestures are the goal here—any of these can be the seed of a choreographic idea.

The middle section, "Workbook," consists of short choreographic prompts. These were assembled over forty years of teaching workshops worldwide (Dublin, Copenhagen, Harvard, and Bard College, among others) and in Rainer's studio art course at the University of California, Irvine, from 2005 to 2013. Each instruction is an open door, a point of departure. Rainer usually grounded her instructions on outside source materials. For example, in her fall 2008 class at the University of California, the phrase "Make a one-minute dance" may have been paired with viewing the 1989 documentary *Home Avenue*. Her journal entry for the class reads,

> Showed *Home Avenue*. Made assignment—deal with the video, or another film/video, another page of text, or combine all three. Katie asked, "How far can we depart from the original source?" I said, "At least touch base with the source, then see where it leads you."

Another journal entry reads, "Distributed five pages from Lethem's *Motherless Brooklyn*. As each read her page aloud, we all took notes, culling actions from the readings." Though not mentioned, this reading could have been paired with the prompt "Make a piece for two people that is subject to psychological interpretation."

Asking the illustrator Pascal Lemaître to supplement the prompts with illustrations was not merely an aesthetic decision. I have been lucky to share my life with him for the past twenty-five years, and so Pascal has seen, recorded, and sketched countless rehearsals and performances. Seeing and following Rainer's work has made a great impression on him. His humorous, sketchlike illustrations in this book remind us to respond to her provocations with visual solutions as well as physical ones. The notebook format invites readers to engage and interact with Rainer's suggestions—annotate, mix and match; relate them to specific course material or projects; add their own voice and the voices of others; find ways to extend, discuss, and challenge the instructions. Jot down ideas freely and without judgment. Play with them.

Finally, the third and last section, "Pedagogical Vaudeville," is a practical example of how to include and transform this material into performance—the specific case in this book was a student performance in Copenhagen in 2000. In this section, Rainer describes how she prepares the terrain before meeting with the participants, and how the material she brings is workshopped, developed, and structured in conversation with the dancers into a final presentation. The process is imperfect and comes with its share of frustrations, as she documents. It also means solving a number of practical problems, dealing with tense relationships, and finding a way to stay true to her initial intentions while being open enough to allow changes to happen. The teaching work of creating a performance means the creator must be alert, seizing opportunities to add new elements to the mix.

Nevertheless: A Workbook is both a primary

source and an interactive document. It is the next closest thing to being in a classroom with one of the most influential artists of the twentieth century. It is a great tool for teaching and an excellent source of inspiration for making original material. We hope that it will help you find (unexpected) moments of poetry. I urge you to do with it what you will: PLAY, with audacity, perseverance, following her methodology.

Conversation

Emmanuèle Phuon: When I started teaching dance improvisation, I was so relieved I could come to you for advice. Then, of course, in the end, you gave me so much more—enough material for this book to come to life. I am always amazed at how generous you are with your time and knowledge.

Let's start with the first section of this book, titled "Nevertheless." What can you tell me about it?

Yvonne Rainer: For a couple of years I taught a class in my loft in what became SoHo for whoever wanted to come—dancers and artists of various sorts. One of the sessions involved some meandering texts which were tape recorded and played as people entered and while I tried to sleep at one end of the space. I paid no attention to what they did. It was a one-shot experiment.

EP: Was this the only text you recorded, or were there others?

YR: I believe that was the only text I recorded. It was for that particular session in my loft.

EP: And what were your motives for ignoring the students? Was that due to the so-called creative freedom of the sixties?

YR: As I said previously, it was a one-shot experiment. It was a way of contesting or complicating my own authority. Or maybe even amplifying it?

EP: You seem uncomfortable with the teacher-student dynamic. Why? You are undeniably an authority in the history of dance. What is, for you, the role of the teacher?

YR: My feelings about teaching changed from year to year, depending on who attended the classes, and whether they were held in my studio or in an academic setting. I don't think I would have attempted the "sleeping professor" experiment in the latter situation. Since my academic classes were for the most part in art departments, and the students were aspiring visual artists, I gave them exercises and compositional problems involving walking, running, dealing with objects, etc. Insofar as most of them were young and reasonably athletic, these basics could be enhanced to include various choreographic and spatial assignments. My most recent teaching experience, however, was in the Barnard Dance Department, where I taught trained dancers an actual piece I had choreographed, *Again? What now?* (2019).

EP: Were the untrained students offered physical practice, such as warmups, before the movement prompts? Or did you encourage them to take technique classes elsewhere? I am asking because you always stress that the Raindears, your current performers, are trained dancers.

And could you please explain the dichotomy between trained and untrained, when you are known for engaging indiscriminately with all levels of movement skills in your pieces?

YR: I don't use them "indiscriminately"; rather, in relation to my own choreographic plans of the moment, like the last piece you were in, *Hellzapoppin': What about the bees?* (2022). This work utilizes traditional dance training in your solos, but most of the piece depends on the ancillary skills that you have acquired along the way, a kind of physical awareness that is an essential byproduct of that training and which gets utilized in all the body contact and lifts. As I indicated previously, I work in a different way with non-dancers. I don't recall ever suggesting that they take dance technique classes.

EP: What do untrained dancers bring to your work versus trained dancers, and why are you interested in using both types?

YR: Untrained performers, especially if they are visual artists, often are very able to be in touch with their bodies in unexpected ways. And they are usually interested in the ways in which my generation of dancers opened up movement possibilities. Adding spatial and temporal concerns to simple actions like walking and running and standing still as a group activity are a start and can lead to other investigations, more specifically focusing on isolating different parts of the body and focusing on improvisation and even sounds and speech. You don't need to be able to balance on half-toe to deal with these kinds of things.

EP: Let's talk about your sources of inspiration. Most students seem to think that ideas fall from the sky, like magic. But I think your work, in particular, has demonstrated that creativity is about being attentive to the world around you, what has been there all along. Your artistic inspiration comes from everyday life—the stuff you do, read, hear, see, etc.

Looking at Pascal Lemaître's illustration for prompt #20, I noticed that he is quoting your dance *RoS Indexical* (2007), when the dancers wore Kleenex boxes instead of shoes. What an unusual image! How did this come about?

YR: Ah so: Kleenex boxes. If I remember correctly, I first used Kleenex boxes in a large group work in the '60s. The performers formed a line at one point and shuffled forward wearing the empty boxes. So at some point in the more recent *RoS Indexical,* the four dancers sit on a sofa and replace their sneakers with the Kleenex boxes and shuffle around until a mob from the audience invades the stage. This latter event indicates my awareness at the time of a possible negative response from a dance audience to the idea of trained dancers "abasing" or negating themselves or the profession to such a degree.

EP: Well, it certainly created a very quirky and memorable image. How can we instill this ability to transpose ideas into strong visuals with students? How do you help them enrich and open their creativity?

YR: I would hope that all the prompts we're publishing in this book entered into my teaching, especially the section titled "Nevertheless," in which I cover multiple possibilities for combining simultaneous movements of different body parts. And, of course, keeping up with what is going on in the dance and performance fields should be a factor, especially if you live in an urban area.

EP: When I used it in my class, I noticed that I was not getting the kind of response one might expect from such inventive and playful instructions. Most dancers are trained to follow instructions scrupulously, and what is produced when they read or hear your instructions are isolated body mechanics. This becomes frustrating for them. How do you work in the classroom to elicit the kind of ingenuity you get from your dancers?

YR: My classroom procedures vary according to the training and experience of the participants, which results in an approach that is very different from working with a consistent group of dancers whose training and experience with me is a constant that I depend on and don't question. I can challenge the latter group with demands that would go over the heads of, say, young, inexperienced art students.

EP: Back to your visual sources. I remember during rehearsals for *Assisted Living—Good Sports 2* (2014) you came in with this huge pile of photographs you had collected from the *New York Times* sports section. You had us pick from the pile randomly and instructed us to link the photos and poses together, making the shortest and most efficient transitions possible between each pose. Definitely a great way to come up with movement material—the challenge residing in how we connected the still images. Does this system come from John Cage and his ideas about indeterminacy?

YR: Photos as source material? I wouldn't say Cage's ideas about chance were the source of this particular idea. In this case, once you learned the sequence of photos, it was set. Lots of dancers of my generation were using photos.

EP: Looking at the journal you kept when teaching at UC Irvine, I see that you assigned Susan Sontag's *Notes on Camp*, the documentary *Coal Miner's Granddaughter* (1991) by Cecilia Dougherty, about a young woman who leaves her Pennsylvania home to find sexual independence in San Francisco, and Eisenstein's films (*Battleship Potemkin*?). Are these sources meant for discussion in class or practical exercises?

YR: Both discussion and sources of inspiration. If the source is a movie, then its use is more obvious: you can adapt actual actions and spatial relationships from it. Literature poses other challenges—turning words into actions or actually reciting text while you are moving—No mystery and no formula required—

EP: In your work, you often interact with the films, texts, and music of other artists by way of quoting, transforming, or juxtaposing. These sources are material to work from, with, and against. Are there books or movies you consider milestones that every student should know?

YR: Aside from Jean Vigo's *Zero for Conduct,* I would recommend anything by Godard, Maya Deren, Kenneth Anger, Hollis Frampton, Germaine Dulac, Robbe-Grillet, René Clair, Buñuel, Cocteau, Dorothy Arzner. As for books, I have just reread two by Elaine Showalter: *Sexual Anarchy: Gender and Culture at the Fin de Siècle* and *The Female Malady: Women, Madness, and English Culture, 1830–1980.* Both especially important for young women artists today in terms of ingenuity and alternatives to madness!

EP: In some of the art programs where I teach, curriculums are less focused on the historical narrative underlying artworks. Young people live in the now, and they want to shape their own aesthetics. Their frame of reference mostly comes from the internet, where everything is up for grabs. But I think it's important for young artists to realize that we all walk in the footsteps of others—there is always a lineage.

Am I right to say, for example, that the dance composition workshop taught at the Cunningham studio from 1962 to 1964 by the musician Robert Dunn—who transposed some of Cage's musical ideas (in turn, often drawn from the artist Marcel Duchamp) into dance—was instrumental in your training? Some Cagean concepts he introduced were silence, translated as stillness; found sounds, interpreted as found movements; and repetition. This differed considerably from more traditional dance composition classes, where students learned to follow musical forms such as AABA or theme and variation. All this is to say that without Duchamp, Cage, Dunn, and a myriad of other artists—those whose works you mention here—Yvonne Rainer would be a different artist!

YR: Absolutely. Dunn's class, with its inclusiveness and permissiveness, was essential to expanding Cunningham's technical teaching. I remember rushing to the windows of the studio and examining movements of people on the street below as though we had never noticed them before. Cage's introduction of everyday sounds in addition to Duchamp's Readymades were primary influences, of course.

EP: And how did the art scene of the '60s—the spontaneous artistic performances known as happenings, or even your relationships with artists such as the painter Robert Rauschenberg or sculptor Robert Morris, contribute to your vision of dance? Do you remember any particular details?

YR: I saw their work, and performed in Morris's work, and both of them performed in some of mine. They knew me, I knew them, I went to see everything they did. Everyone went to see everything everybody else did. You know, the late '50s and early '60s were such a hotbed of ideas. The audiences at these happenings and Judson concerts, the Cage concerts, openings of artists' work at the Green Gallery—the audiences were much smaller. You saw the same people all the time. So it's hard to say who explicitly influenced whom. All these ideas were thrown up and came down, landing on different people in different ways.

EP: It seems to me that your playful approach encourages critical thinking by keeping a healthy distance from the "agonizing" creative process. In the "Workbook" section of this book, your prompts paired with Pascal's drawings bring up this aspect of your work and personality that few people have had the chance to experience firsthand. How do you bring humor and play to your dance work and in the classroom?

YR: That's also hard to answer. I don't recall ever explicitly assigning "Make a funny dance." But now I'm remembering some rehearsals at Barnard for the dance I taught there. At one point, in order to relieve a long unison event, I had two people break out from it, one of them fleeing from the other, who was impersonating a monster. I had asked for two volunteers, one of whom wasn't very convincing as "the monster," so I asked someone else, who turned out to be great. At another point during the *Chair-Pillow* (1969) finale, when some of the performers are sitting still in their chairs, one of them yawned, and I asked her to do it in performance. She did. I always try to be sensitive to spontaneous behavior during rehearsals and incorporate it into the final show. Sometimes it's funny and sometimes simply a distraction.

EP: The goal in combining the illustrations with your prompts is to alert the reader to the situations you mention here. Pascal Lemaître's drawings remind us to play, joke, explore spontaneous behavior, take inspiration in everyday life actions, no matter how prosaic. They challenge readers to distance themselves from an overly academic or literal approach. So much has been written about you and your work, people forget you are first and foremost an artist—not a dance theorist.

This brings me to my question: What makes you laugh? Are there any "funny" scenes in your work?

YR: Everywhere, from noticing and incorporating a performer's yawn in rehearsal to using excerpts from Laurel and Hardy or Jacques Tati. I was always alert to the whimsical and irreverent in my daily life and aesthetic perusals.

EP: I am looking at Barnard College's website: you were the Lida A. Orzeck '68 Distinguished Artist-in-Residence for 2019. As a women's college, Barnard's mission statement has been described as "focusing on empowering young women to become even more exceptional."

Just curious: any specific material you brought to address this topic?

YR: That's hard to answer because that quote was not of my making! "Empowering young women" was not one of my primary concerns, although the students I ended up working with were all women. If male Columbia students had been interested in working with me, I would have accepted them. In any teaching situation, I have to assume that whatever I have to offer will be picked up by some or most of the students.

EP: Also on the website: "At Barnard, we challenge you to stand out and take risks. We encourage you to be unafraid. We champion your independence as you try, fail, learn, refine, and ultimately discover how to make your mark." How would you explain risk-taking to a young student today?

YR: Another difficult question. Maybe just remaining true to your initial inspirations and assumptions, either to sustain them or to challenge them. It's also important to find contemporaries in the same boat in order to avoid isolation. I am fully aware that economically, most aspiring choreographers will have a much more difficult time maintaining a career than I did in the '60s and '70s. A young neighbor of mine doesn't even go to class anymore, can't afford it! I recall that in my generation of aspiring artists and dancers, we talked mainly about art and dance history and maybe current politics, whereas now it seems to be more about rents and ways to make a living.

EP: Did you learn anything from these young women?

YR: Of course! Besides their initial interest in what I have to offer, there's always a challenge that goes with it, in the form of their questions and humor, all of which KEEPS ME ON MY TOES. Teaching and rehearsing constitute an ongoing interactive process, always full of surprises.

EP: The last section of this book, "Pedagogical Vaudeville"—what a great title—is a journal that describes the process of turning a workshop into a performance. Here we see very clearly how you transform life into art. Vaudevilles are performances made up of a series of separate, unrelated acts grouped together. And indeed, so many different things happen during the workshop. Who shows up and when, what material they come up with based on your prompts, the various conversations they engage in, the ways they deal with the available space. You integrate all of it into the performance that you present at the end of the workshop.

I am curious, how do you bring all these elements together? Is there a method, do you write or storyboard it?

YR: When I have been invited to do a workshop anywhere, I devise a series of rudimentary suggestions and go from there. Then, depending on the duration of the gig and the allotted space and the inclinations of the participants, hopefully some kind of performance will emerge, as it did when I was invited to the Danish Academy of Art in Copenhagen in 2000 to work with art students. One thing I recall from that particular workshop is a moment when some of the participants wanted to improvise outdoors in a courtyard. Given the brevity of my stay there, I had to dissuade them from such an idea. It eventually all took place in two adjacent indoor rooms. Or maybe the reason for my censure was that I have never liked working outdoors! Another reservation probably was that dealing with students and improvisation takes time, and I was there for only five days. In any case, I eventually arrived with a set of ideas, some of which were taken up, some not.

EP: "Measure the room with your body; define 'happening'; define 'modern dance'; describe a scene from a movie that impressed you." All great prompts to work from!

But my question pertains to how you arrange the material the students produce. How do you decide what goes where and when? What advice would you give your students regarding choreographic structure?

YR: "Structure" can either emerge from content or create content. "Make a one-minute dance" is a "structural" instruction. "Roll your head while patting your abdomen" is content. Both can be combined by rolling dice, aesthetic choice, or specific stratagems depending on the source material for a particular piece of choreography, such as the jitterbug section of the Hollywood film *Hellzapoppin'*, my last choreographic venture.

EP: I am looking at a diagram your partner, the art historian and theorist Martha Gever, created to differentiate modernism from postmodernism. It was part of the same journal I mentioned earlier, the one you kept while teaching at UC Irvine. Martha was teaching there at the same time too. It's remarkable!

Nov. 3rd, 2008

Modernity	Postmodernity
balance	~~complexity~~
stability	chaos
moral law	disjunction
continuity	fragmentation
organic	simulation
depth	rupture
substance	surface
flow	collision
coherence	contestation
authenticity	style
harmony → dissonance	artificial/
integration → disruption	structed

assign Notes on Camp
Coalminers' Granddaughter
Eisenstein

objectivity ⟶ multi-subjecti

YR: Wow, I had totally forgotten about that! Martha sure summed up the postmodern mission. Whether or not her convoluted diagram influenced me, I was certainly aware of the importance of contesting previous certainties in the arts, especially performance. But I don't recall if I used her ingenious illustration. The pairs that stand out for me are stability/collision, continuity/rupture, flow/disjunction, and coherence/fragmentation.

EP: Do you come to the studio with prepared material, or do you leave it up to what you see in rehearsal in your performers' responses?

YR: Both, of course. I am always open to what my performers come up with. Like in *Hellzapoppin'*, I was so delighted with my performers' solutions to adapting the Hollywood film sequence that I had no additional need to revise what they did.

EP: With the emergence of AI, grounding art-making in the body and insisting on the valuable experience of doing and being will become more and more essential. I am reading an interview with Vera Broido, the Dada artist Raoul Hausmann's lover. According to her, Hausmann believed that all forms of creative expression are tied together, and that all arts (architecture, music, literature) begin with dance, the body in movement.

Do you encourage your students to think that art can change the world? For you, what is the place of dance in the continuum of the art world?

YR: I don't recall anyone ever asking me that question! But I would NEVER declare that art can change the world. Artists make changes in art, at times BIG ones, and in that respect I am ambitious. Outside of my profession, I donate money and join protest marches and hope that such actions will support causes like climate change, feminism, anti-racism, anti-Trumpism, et al.

EP: Our illustrator Pascal Lemaître, also a teacher, has two questions for you: Has your experience in filmmaking changed the way you choreograph? and, Do you view teaching as a political act?

YR: Apropos of filmmaking: I turned to film to deal with specific social and political subject matter, and when I returned to dance around 1999, I found ways to combine the language of political issues alongside my choreography, mainly by my presence as a reader or through voice-over. The choreographic ideas didn't change that much. As to the second question, it certainly depends on what and how you teach. The classroom can expose students to new possibilities in terms of subject matter, techniques, resources, movement, voice, and more. It is hard at this point to do much more than generalize. If politics is a way of thinking about change, then one can see all art as political. Unfortunately, I don't foresee Trump getting his comeuppance as a consequence of my artmaking OR my teaching!

EP: In 2022, during a public conversation with the choreographer Bill T. Jones after one of our performances, a student asked, "What can this generation of artists do to break the status quo?"

What would be your answer today? From my perspective, your generation has opened so many doors. What's left to do?

YR: There is always more to do! I can only encourage them to begin again.

Part 1

Nevertheless

*Nevertheless, we do need to do specific exercise-type things now & then, so the challenge is to make an exercise situation.

I DON'T LIKE BEING UP HERE!

Western teaching.

I really don't like being up here; I don't like this kind of separation. I like the idea of creating a situation & becoming a part of it along with the rest of you.* Of course the classical Western teaching mode is also a situation—if unacknowledged as such—with the teacher demonstrating and then correcting: a little talk, a little dance, a little teach. I am not convinced this is the only way one can learn about one's body. The Balinese strap the young onto the master's back. Whatever the method, the process of awareness is slow. I am going to try something different. I am going to launch two distinct & separate entities into this space: this tape, with its mélange of instructions, explanations, and rationalizations, and my body with what I hope will be a continuity of focus & involvement. You have about 3 choices— no, 4,—no, 5. You can listen, or you can look, or you can listen and look—actually you have hundreds of choices: you can try to remember & do all of the things I am doing, or only 3 or 2 or 1; you can try to remember & do all of the things I suggest you do, or only 3, etc. Sometimes I shall follow

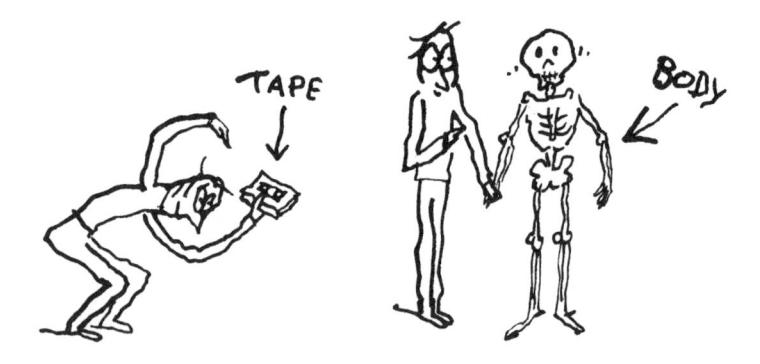

my own instructions, sometimes not. The important thing to remember is that the circulations of these ideas from this tape and from this body have very specific and calculated limitations and so can be understood as a means thru which you can explore your own bodies during this time and in this place & with these particular people and at your own pace. Those of you who are somewhat familiar with your own bodies and those of you who have studied with me before may have more ease with this procedure than others of you, who may flounder. Don't worry: floundering can be useful. I shall devote a certain portion of the time to flounders. I shall play this tape over & over. We shall at times flounder together. Floundering is better than foundering. It is not possible to founder simply because we are all here in the world, in this room, in each other's minds, supported & connected by thought and space.

Most parts of the body can move independently. Many parts of the body can move simultaneously, if only at random. We run into difficulty when we start categorizing simple motions & try playing one kind against another. The classic example is patting your head with one hand & rubbing your belly with the other. Since one can pat and rub with only the hands & feet—and possibly the elbows. I have devised broader categories to describe motion—circular, back & forth, up & down, side to side—these can be applied to almost all parts of

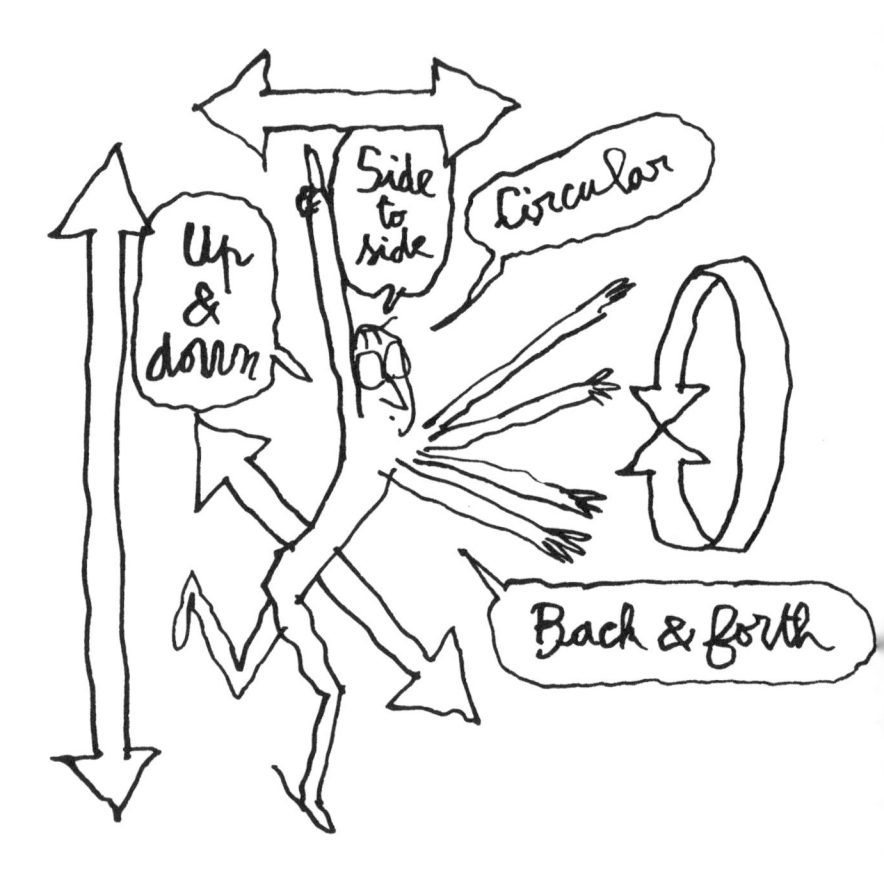

the body, in addition to the specialized terms that can be used for the back and torso: like slump, slouch, curve, bend, compress—all of which can be alternated with expand, straighten, or enlarge. I'll probably think of others as I go along. I am eliminating sequences that consist of more than two elements: like pat your head then slump your back then straighten your back then bend your knees, etc. That gets into the area of the dancer's memory and I'm not here to put any more of that into the world than I can help; I figure I've done my share. I am more interested in an immediate simultaneous kind of continuity that anybody can master & keep going once you get the hang of it. Let's start at the top. The head can move up & down as in nodding; it can move from side to side as in saying no; it can move from side to side alternating left ear to left shoulder & right ear to right shoulder; it can revolve circularly in either direction. The ears can wiggle but what do you think we are—a bunch of kids? The shoulders can go up & down, backward & forward; they can revolve forward & revolve backward. Since there are two of them, they can work in unison, they can do any one thing in opposing directions—like revolve one shoulder forward & the other one backward, move one up when the other moves down, move one forward while the other moves backward. This last maneuver does funny things with the shoulder blades & makes one start wanting to do the rib cage. Hold off. We're still on shoulders. Can you revolve one while the other moves up & down? Can you move one up and down while the other moves back & forth? Can you revolve one shoulder while the other moves back & forth? The head and shoulders can move simultaneously. The head can move up & down while the shoulders do likewise. There are many variations in rhythm possible here—like 2 shoulder cycles to one of head & vice versa. The shoulders can move in opposing directions while the head moves up & down. I think the picture is beginning to emerge: I have listed 4 possibilities for head and 9 for shoulders, which makes 36 possibilities for combining head and shoulders. Forget about your dandruff. The easiest combinations consist only of circular movements or only of back & forth-type movements. To combine both circular & back & forth is to teeter over the abyss. There is a shoulder possibility I overlooked: revolve both forward but alternately, likewise backward. When multiplied by the 4 head movements there are now a total of 44 combinations. If we worked out all 44 tonight, we would never, any of us, move our shoulders or heads again.

Arms. The arms bend & straighten. They bend with the elbows down, forward, side or back and all kinds of degrees in between. They can straighten in almost any direction. Straight they can move in practically any two directions in unison, in opposition, or alternately. Depending on how loose your shoulder joints are, they can revolve on an axis extending from your collar bone both forward & backward almost 360 degrees. A suggestion: Extend your arms straight to the side just below shoulder level; bring them straight forward on the same plane so that they are parallel. Bring them back to the side. Now alternate so that when one moves to the front the other is to the side, etc. Are you sure they are isolated or are you also moving your torso? It is obviously impossible to classify all the possibilities for the arms and besides it's one o'clock in the morning and the cat is on a rampage. There are innumerable circular movements for straight arms in all positions & for forearms alone when the arms are bent. Hands. I won't even talk about them. Can you roll your head & swing your arms? Can you revolve your shoulders, arms, & head at the same time? Can you

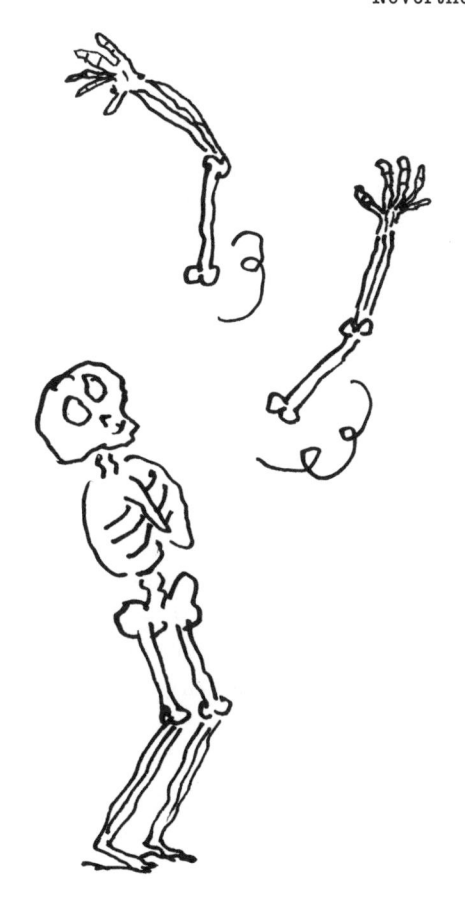

bend & straighten your arms, move your shoulders up and down, & move your head side to side ear to shoulder—all simultaneously? How about rolling your head & making large circles with straight arms?

Let's forget about the head and shoulders for a while, as they must be tired, but remember the arms & focus on the torso. The torso can slump as in a bad posture chart—an S-curve indented at the small of the back & rounded forward at the level of the shoulder blades. Make sure your shoulders are relaxed: this position has nothing to do with the shoulders. The torso can straighten out of this position. The S-curve can be assumed laterally, or from side to side. That is, the rib cage can move by itself from side to side on a plane parallel to the floor. It can take the shoulders with it, or the shoulders can stay put; this last is very tricky & greatly reduces the range of movement. Once you start playing around you will find that the rib cage is a very mobile member of the body. It is capable of incredibly small, subtle motions. By compressing the diaphragm, you can drop the rib cage vertically down; you can rotate it on a vertical axis in either direction; you can do a figure 8 on that same axis; you can alternately rotate one side at a time forward or backward; you can alternately raise & lower each side without extending beyond the vertical plane of the body. The term torso covers more ground, excuse me—body, taking in the spine & midsection. The torso can bend beyond the vertical plane of the body in all directions & return. This movement can involve only the upper torso—including the upper spine & breastbone—& head, or it can call into play the whole spine all the way to the pelvis. In side & forward directions the torso can slump <u>into</u> itself and also in a larger arc <u>out</u> of itself. For instance, moving forward you can collapse your midsection so that the upper spine is curved forward but <u>behind</u> the normal vertical plane of the body, or you can lift your midsection to facilitate rounding the spine forward in a larger arc & totally in front of the normal vertical plane of the body. Can you go from one to the other? Can you go from one to the other while swinging your arms? Can you go from one to the other while swinging your arms and nodding your head? Can you go from one to the other

while bending & straightening your knees? The
torso can bend to the side & while there can collapse forward or round forward. Collapse forward
and round forward. Perhaps I should say collapse
forward & arch forward: arch in the sense of a Ro-
manesque archway. Collapse forward & arch forward. Collapse sideways, straighten, then arch
sideways. My back is not flexible enuf to do this
to the rear. You might try working it out for your-
selves. Collapse sideways, then collapse forward.
Straighten up. Arch sideways then arch forward.
In all these torso maneuvers, the head can go with
the spine or oppose it in some way; it can stay
straight in relation to the room & normal right-
side-up vision, or it can stay straight in relation to
the spine. The world is upside down when we are
upside down. Just think of the control we would
have if our eyeballs revolved in our heads to adjust
to askew positions of the head. Or would that be
confusing: to stand on one's hands & see the world

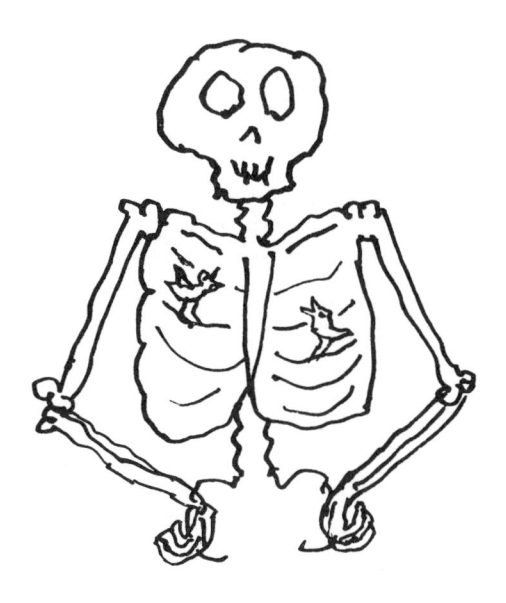

right-side-up? They might get stuck so that when
you stood up again the world would be upside down
for the rest of one's life. Better not to think of such
things. Arch sideways, then rotate the rib cage laterally in relation to itself. Do this again after arch-
ing sideways then forward. You will notice that
the rib cage has much more mobility in an arched
position than in a collapsed position. Which says
something about breathing and the ability of the
lungs to expand in an expanded chest as opposed
to a collapsed chest. Not that one wants to expand
the lungs in New York. But in case an opportu-
nity arises you'll know how to do it. I am probably
talking too fast for you to attempt all of the things
I am suggesting, so I will pause here & interject

some reminders and reassurances. The tape will
be played over & over; what you don't hear on one
round you'll catch on the next. I am talking about
the skeleton, not about muscles, even though one
obviously exerts muscle energy in order to manip-
ulate bones. I don't know much about muscles: only
that when you work them too much they blow up
& make you feel constipated. Leave them alone &
they'll come home & do what you want them to do.
I could concentrate on the buttocks, for instance.
There are strippers who can make each buttock revolve in a different direction; also the breasts. But
these feats are for the virtuosically inclined, in the
same class as wiggling the ears. I have more mod-
est ambitions. Then there is the matter of rhythm.
All of these movements are what I call 2-beat
movements in that most of them have only 2 parts

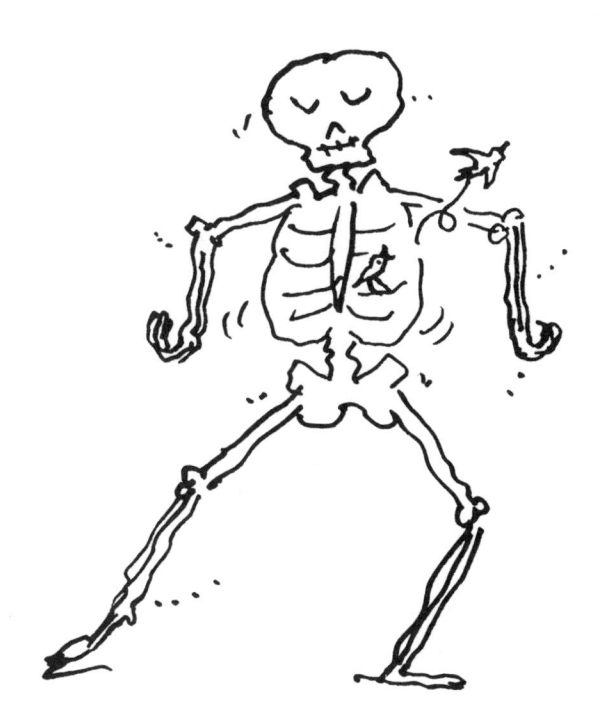

and are small enuf to take place within a 2-count or roughly 2-second duration. & sometimes 2 half-seconds. When you start putting 3 of them together & each one's tempo varies slightly, you get a jazz-ier look. Like bend & straighten your knees & arms & nod your head.

Hips or pelvis. No, one last thing about rib cage: try revolving your rib cage on a horizontal axis. Pelvis can revolve on a vertical axis; it can tilt for-ward & back; it can move from side to side. With the aid of the legs & feet, it can do a figure 8 for-ward & backward. Most large movements of the pelvis are facilitated by the legs simply because it is not free-floating like the rib cage but is sup-ported directly from underneath by its underpin-nings the legs. When combined with the torso, the range of both is vastly increased. Try touching your right shoulder to your right hip. Move your rib cage to the side; see how much farther you can go when the pelvis moves to the other side. Move your pelvis diagonally forward & diagonally back. What happens when you arch your torso forward & then revolve your pelvis? Do you find that when the pelvis is in the forward part of the revolution the torso automatically is in a collapsed position? Can you revolve your pelvis & rotate your arms in some fashion? Can you move the pelvis from side to side & nod your head? For some reason, that's a strange one. Shaking the head seems easier. How about shaking the head, i.e., moving it from side to side, & revolving the pelvis? Somehow moving the head & pelvis at the same time makes a no-man's-land out of the torso. How about revolving both head and pelvis simultaneously? Can you open & shut your mouth while doing that? Another inter-jection: What happens when you get as close as you can to another person & try to do some of this stuff? Stand back-to-back, decide who is leader & try to decipher physically what the other guy is doing. I don't have much more time; it is almost 6 PM & you will all be arriving soon.

I haven't said a word about the legs & covering space. Actually, I haven't much use for the legs except as they hold up our bodies. More about that next week.

Oct 2

Tonight's class starts as soon as you come in the door. It started with arrival of the first two people. Half the class is audience and the other half performer. That is the first thing you must decide on the basis of half & half. If you are audience, sit or stand along the wall against which the mirror is leaning. If you are performer, listen to the tape & make your decisions. If you get

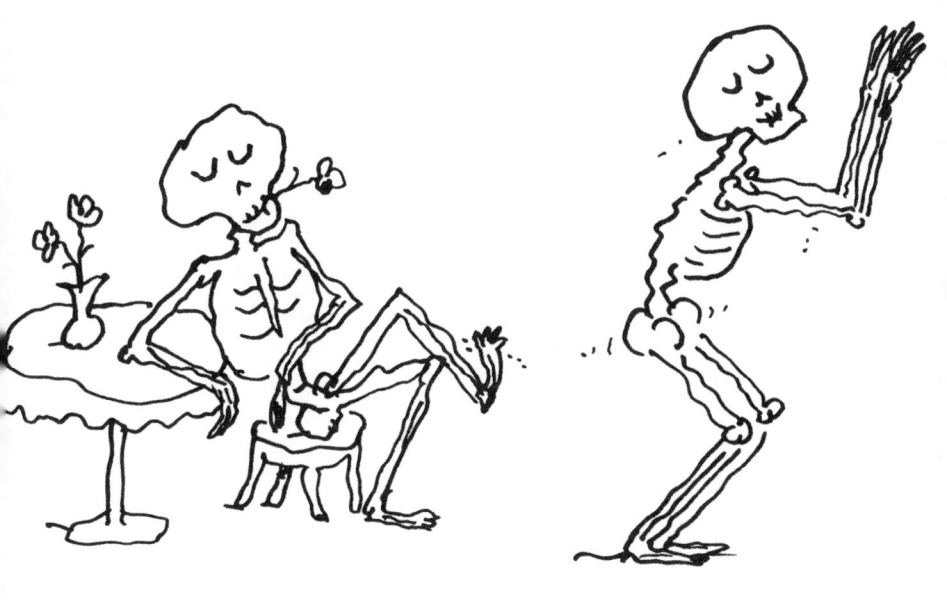

tired of being a performer, go to a member of the
audience & change roles, communicating to him
that you are doing so. First rule for performers
is that they must keep in motion. I shall not specify the style or type of movement. Remember that
at least at the beginning you must also be able to
listen to this tape. The content of this class shall
be bodies—animate and inanimate. The object-
like ties in this room occupy a given amount of
space, and the placement of each determines the
exact amount of empty space available for movement or for redistribution of these same objects.
Our bodies—despite the difference that lies in the
fact of our volition—can be looked at in the same

manner. We occupy space; when one of us moves out of that space he leaves room for another to enter or for an inanimate object to be placed there. This room is chock full of redistributable material. Since I have a bad leg, I have made a decision tonight not to move of my own volition other than to rewind the tape. Consequently, on one level I am making my body equivalent to the redistributable inanimate objects in this room. The audi-

ence can be regarded and dealt with in similar fashion. I advise you not to struggle with material that is too heavy for you but to ask for assistance from fellow participants if you need it. Remember that you must keep moving, even while listening & even while talking. The session will be over when all the material is returned to its original placement, including audience. So, if you start out being audience, you will end up being audience. I think that the first thing to do is to take stock of exactly where everything is, especially of those things that you might be interested in moving. Exactly how are they situated, what is the distance between the nearest objects, how many steps is it from a particular object to its nearest neighbor, how many steps is it from a particular object to one most distant from it? How many steps are required from a particular member of the audience to the nearest object? I suggest you take several of these measurements, try to remember them & recheck them at the end of the evening. Remember that we are dealing with distributable material, i.e. the columns don't count, partitions don't count, doorknobs don't count. I would prefer that you refrain from asking me questions during the session but try to figure out a mode of operating by listening to the tape and observing your fellow participants. If there are serious omissions in these instructions, they will have to be discussed at the end of the session.

*Nevertheless we do need to do specific exercise-type things now & than, so the challenge is to make an exercise situation.

I really don't like being up here; I don't like this kind of separation. I like the idea of creating a situation & becoming a part of it along with the rest of you.* Of course the classical western teaching mode is also a situation - if unacknowledged as such - with the teacher demonstrating and then correcting: a little talk, a little dance, a little teach. I am not convinced this is the only way one can learn about one's body. The Balinese strap the young onto the master's back. Whatever the method the process of awareness is slow. I am going to try something different. I am going to launch two distinct & separate entities into this space: this tape with its melange of instructions, explanations and rationalizations, and my body with what I hope will be a continuity of focus & involvement. You have about 3 choices -- no, 4 -- no, 5 -- You can listen, or you can look, or you can listen and look, --actually you have hundreds of choices: you can try to ~~maxail~~ remember & do all of the things I am doing, or only 3 or 2 or 1; you can try to remember & do all of the things I suggest you do, or only 3, etc. Sometimes I shall follow my own instructions, sometimes not. The important thing to remember is that the circulations of these ideas ~~x~~ from this tape and from this body have very specific ~~limitations~~ and calculated limitations and so can be understood as a means thru which you can explore your own bodies during this time and in this place & with these particular people and at your own pace. Those of you who are somewhat familiar with your own bodies and those of you who have studied with me before may have more ease with this procedure than others of you, who may flounder. Don't worry: floundering ~~x~~ can be useful. I shall devote a certain portion of the time to flounders. I shall play this tape over & over. We shall at times flounder together. Floundering is better than foundering. It is not possible to founder simply because we are all here in the world,

Most parts of the body can move independently. Many parts of the body can move simultaneously, if only at random. We run into difficulty when we start catagorizing simple motions & try playing one kind against the other. The classic example in this room, in eac other's minds, supported & connected by thought and space. is patting your head with one hand & rubbing your belly with the other. Since one can't pat and rub with only the hands & feet - and possibly the elbows - I have devised broader categories to describe motion - circular, back & forth, up & down, side to side - these can be applied to almost all parts of the body, in addition to the specialized terms that can be used for the back and torse: like slump, slouch, curve, bend, compress - all of which can be alternated with expand, straightan, or enlarge. I'll probably think of others as I go along. I am eliminating sequences that consist of more than two elements: like pat your head then slump your ~~x~~ back then straightn your back then bend your knees, etc. That gets into the area of the dancer's memory and I'm not here to put any more of that into the world than I can help; I figure I've done my share. I am more interested in an immediate simultaneous kind of continuity that anybody can master & keep going once you get the hang of it. Let's start at the top. The head can move up & down as in nodding; it can move from side to side as in saying no; it can move from side to side alternating left ear to left shoulder & right ear to right shoulder; it can revolve circularly in either direction. The ears can wiggle but what do you think we are - a bunch of kids!? The shoulders can go up & down, backward & forward; they can revolve forward & revolve backward. Since there are two of them they can work in unison, they can do any one thing in opposing directions - like revolve one shoulder forward & the other one backward, move one up when the other moves down, move one forward while the other moves backward. This last manoeuver does funny things with the shoulder blades & makes one start wanting to do the rib cage. Hold off. We're

Part 2
Workbook

1. Make a one-minute dance.

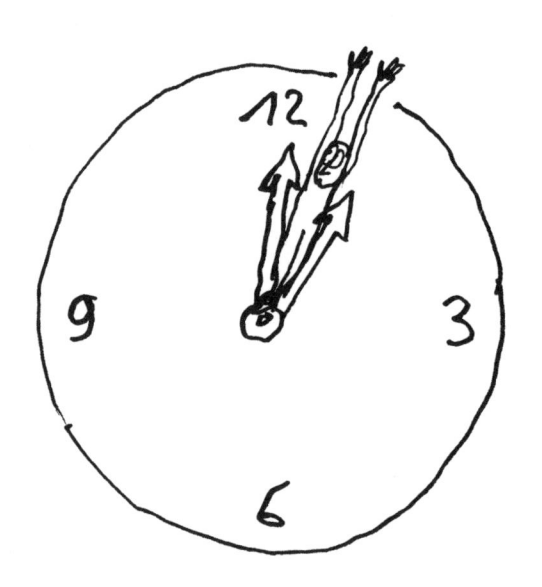

2. Make a piece for this space.

Notes

3. Make a piece for some other space and make the getting there part of the piece.

Notes

4. Make a piece from observing intimately any five-minute period of your own behavior during the day. (No pantomime.)

5. Observe a two- to five-minute segment of someone else's behavior and perform it. (No pantomime.)

6. Improvise spontaneously and emphasize one of the following:

Time Body Light Rhythm Place Activity
Changes Transitions Energy Performance
Sound Characterization Space Movement
Speed Situation.

7. Prepare a piece that does the above.

8. Make a complicated
two-minute piece.

9. Make a simple two-minute piece.

10. Deal with an object in a
symbolic manner.

11. In a non-symbolic manner.

12. Make a piece for two
people that is subject
to psychological
interpretation.

Notes

13. Make a piece for
two people that is not
subject to psychological
interpretation.

14. Make an hour-long piece
that can take place during
other performances
(without interfering).

15. Prepare a repetitive
interference mode
and perform it during
someone's piece.

16. Make a continuous phrase
(i.e., one in which the
end can merge into the
beginning without pause)
that can be repeated for
an hour.

17. Make a 3-minute disjointed piece.

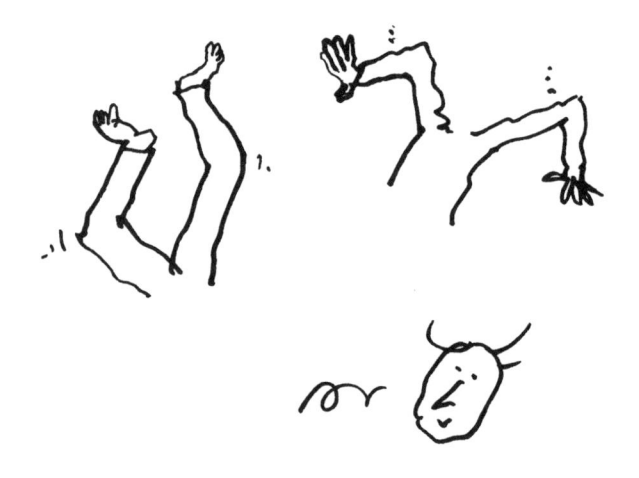

Notes

18. Make a 30-second
disjointed piece.

19. Make two short pieces that can be performed simultaneously and that have nothing to do with each other.

20. Present two simultaneous
performances that have
some connection—either
actual or metaphorical.

21. Present something you really dig.

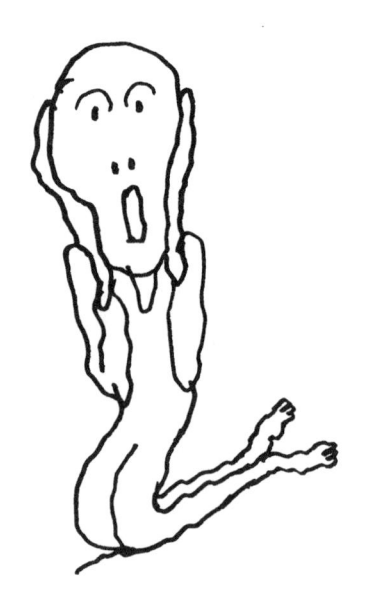

22. Do something that feels
alien to you.

23. Make a piece that
contains both functional
and nonfunctional
activities.

24. Make an extremely short
work for an extremely
large group. If it cannot
be executed, tell us
about it.

25. Make a funny dance.

26. Teach material to one or more others—as a performance.

27. Make a piece involving rules governing competition (games).

28. Make a work that
<u>must</u> take place amidst
the observers (and
nowhere else).

29. Do anything you want (at your own risk).

30. Spontaneously and as
quickly as you can,
do 25 different things.

31. Spontaneously and
as slowly as you can,
do 5 different things.

Notes

32. Make 10 different things
and determine by chance
how long each is going
to last.

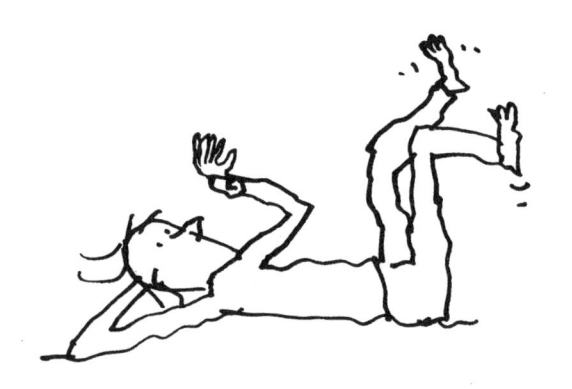

33. Do #32 and distribute
the actions or activities
among 12 people.

34. Do #33 and distribute
the 10 durations
over 5 minutes; over
60 seconds.

Notes

35. Make a piece involving
corresponding progressions
in distance, speed, and
duration: e.g., near to far;
short to long (distance);
slow to fast; short to long
(time); etc.

36. Make something that has
no transitions.

37. Make a solo involving characterization other than your own.

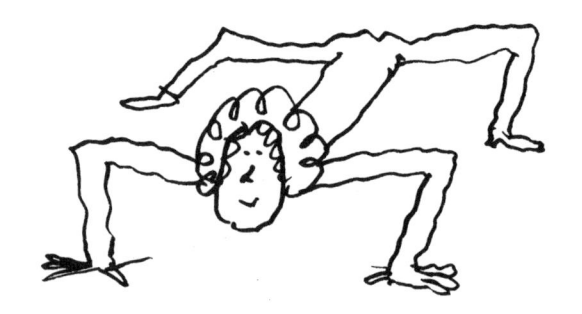

38. Make something that involves actual contact with another or others.

39. Travel a long distance
as fast as you can
while making regular
changes in your means
of locomotion.

40. Do any of the above;
then reverse exactly.

41. Do any of the above while carrying on a monologue or a conversation with someone (either prepared or spontaneous).

42. By any random or chance
means (numbers out of a
hat, telephone directory,
dice, coins, etc.) determine
first the total number
of these directives to
combine in one piece;
then (also by chance)
determine the particular
ones that will comprise
the piece.

43. Do #42 using choice
rather than chance.

Notes

44. Collaborate on any of the above.

45. Ask a few other people
to discuss collaborating
on any of the above and
present the discussion
as performance (either
prepared—via tape and/or
memorized transcript—
or spontaneous).

46. Incorporate a headline from the *New York Times* by voice into any of the above.

"WE BELIEVE THAT GREAT JOURNALISM HAS THE POWER TO MAKE EACH READER'S LIFE RICHER AND MORE FULFILLING, AND ALL OF SOCIETY STRONGER AND MORE JUST."

47. If you are male, recite a section of a feminist news article or essay along with your movement sequence.

48. If you are female,
approach a male soloist
and ask him what he's
been reading.

49. While you are performing any of the foregoing tasks, tell us what you think of Donald Trump.

50. Incorporate a brief
autobiographical narrative
into your movement
sequence, especially if
you are performing close
to others.

Part 3
Pedagogical Vaudeville

Pedagogical Vaudeville was a performance by Danish art students that resulted from a workshop that I conducted in Copenhagen at the invitation of Yvette Brackman, an American performance artist who was teaching at the Danish Academy of Art. A preliminary correspondence between us set the stage for the materials and ideas I would provide for the students in preparation for the final event, which took place on April 14, 2000.

What is unique about this document is that—choreographically, architecturally, and socially—it involves a process that I have never recorded in such detail as it went along, before or since! My more recent choreographic ventures, on the other hand, entail a more calculated kind of "cherry-picking" from decades of work, and are not geared to discovery each time with a new group of performers—the Raindears, my current group, more simply, are accustomed to executing a somewhat predetermined script. There is also the difference between working with professional dancers and with art students who had no performing experience. The latter instance creates more of a workshop than a series of professional rehearsals, with the result that in Copenhagen I felt I had to bring in "ideas" rather than predetermined moves that they, for the most part, would have been ill-equipped to execute.

The other difference between my "professional" custom and the Copenhagen situation was the unforeseen and nontraditional nature of the Danish Academy performance space itself—i.e., the two rooms that ultimately became our unlikely base of operations—in contrast to the more conventional spaces the Raindears are used to, which create a kind of "Readymade" in terms of audience positioning and framing.

Furthermore, my dance group's professionalism prompts an entirely different range of possibilities. The comparison raises questions of modern-dance history in relation to "postmodern" improvisation and accident, although after Copenhagen I have cited my subsequent choreographies as examples of my own postmodernism. Ha! What passes for avant-garde for one generation is "merely modern" at another historical moment, albeit in this case, perhaps, in reverse chronological order—the earlier (Danish) performance of 2000 seeming more "avant-garde" or postmodern than the dances created in the ensuing eighteen years! It might be interesting for someone—YOU?—to use the Pedagogical Vaudeville diary as a score for an entirely new dance! Be my guest.

Preliminary email correspondence with Yvette Brackman and Karena Nomi

January 15, 2000
Dear Yvette:
It would necessarily be a quite short performance, and I would have to send instructions/as-
signments beforehand, such as:
Prepare a 1- to 4-minute presentation derived
from 1) what you have recently or are currently
reading; 2) the last movie you saw; or 3) a "situation" (invented or based on fact).
I purposely use the term "presentation" and do
not specify the medium. It can be as simple as the
reading of a text or as complicated as the time and
place of presentation allows. One stipulation: no
pantomime!
Yvonne

March 16, 2000
Dear Yvette:
I am sending the Noel Carroll text to the school,
attention of Ida Pagh Davidsen. In answer to your
questions:
To avoid a bunch of solo "acts" each student
should—individually—think about how many people he or she wants as part of her/his presentation and enlist the necessary cooperation. Any one
of these could conceivably be a solo or involve as
many as the whole group. No single presentation—
by individual or individuals—should be more than
three minutes. I think 15 people is the maximum
number of participants. So there is the potential
for 15 presentations. The medium is up to them:
live/recorded speech, live action, video, film, dis-

cussion, recitation, reading, description of yet-to-be-realized presentation. More than one presentation can happen at a time.

I must constantly remind myself of the value of mistakes, failures, interruptions, breakdowns, interferences, accidents, incompletions, muddles, mix-ups . . . and chance occurrences. They don't have to totally organize everything. They don't have to reveal everything to each other. They can surprise each other . . . and me. Have fun.

Yvonne

The students, through a representative, Karena Nomi, wrote me to propose that the workshop theme be the idea of "the good life," and asked if I wanted them to prepare work around a common theme.

March 27, 2000

Dear Students:

The problem with a "common theme" is that it runs the risk of propelling your work as a group into conventional structures of development and resolution. It is easier to fall into this trap than you may think. I myself am more interested in heterogeneity than homogeneity. But "the good life" sounds like a terrific idea. What is it, who is offering it, what are our expectations of it, how is desire organized, expressed, or, as the case may be, suppressed? I think, therefore I shop (to paraphrase Barbara Kruger). Etc., etc. What is "the bad life?" What are you reading?

As for methods of working, can you think along the lines of how each of you, individually, wants to use anywhere from one to 15 people in any single presentation or segment? One factor may be the social composition of the group. Do you all know each other? Have you worked with each other before? Would someone prefer to be behind a video camera to document your discussions, which in turn might constitute a segment of the whole or might provide a "template" from which you could "re-enact" parts of discussions? These are my free-association ramblings. Use them as you see fit.

And keep in touch. Best, Yvonne—I look forward to meeting all of you.

Sunday

Karena meets me at the airport and takes me by taxi to the hotel several blocks from the Academy. In response to my questions, she tells me she has studied ballet and modern dance before enrolling at the Academy. She points out various sights, most interesting is Christiana, the former naval base that has been a squatters' settlement since the early 70s.

I crash for several hours, then prepare to meet Yvette Brackman and Amy Sillman for dinner. Amy, a very talented painter whose exhibition I have just seen in New York and immensely liked, has been teaching here for a week and will stay on for another week. I am looking forward to seeing her in this context. There is a knock at my door. It is Amy, in all her usual exuberance. The three of us have dinner near the harbor. Yvette is the recently appointed American director of the "Mur og Rum" ("Walls and Spaces") School, an autonomous entity within the Academy. She explains the workings and structure of the Academy. I describe my correspondence and taxi ride with Karena. Yvette tells me that Karena, who is a first-year student, had been accepted on the basis of her art submission, a large blue-screen blue cube. We marvel at the gutsiness of a dancer to make such a bold move.

Amy suggests a collaboration. She has assigned her painting students the task of making large painted balls, about a yard in diameter. Could they be used in the performance? I immediately pounce on the idea of having them rolled into the space during the show. Both she and Amy smoke after dinner. It's been a long time since I was last exposed to European smoking culture. No repairing to the bar area in this neck of the world. Later that night my jet-lag keeps me awake for several hours. I make the following jottings on individual slips of paper from a note-pad:

Move as slowly as you can throughout this session.
Measure the room with your body.
Define "happening."
Define "modern dance."
Describe a scene from a movie that impressed you.
Execute unaccustomed activities with a chair.
Describe a walk in the city.

In rapid succession, perform static poses that express or are in response to the following:

I am in despair.
I love you.
Why don't you love me?
Why are you abusing me?
I am enraged at you.
You abandoned me!
Why did you leave me?
I'm gay.
I thought you'd never come.

I long for you.

I'm scared.

Don't be scared.

I am overjoyed.

Make a list of gestures as you observe them during the
first session, then perform them in the same order.

Monday

We convene in a large room off of a cobble-
stoned courtyard which is enclosed on four sides by
the imposing facades of an 18th century palace. As
the students arrive, I give each of them one of the
slips of paper.

Yvette has already informed me that the workshop will take place elsewhere. When everyone—at
this point, nine women and two men—has arrived,
we walk across the courtyard, splitting halfway
into two groups. One group has moved toward
the main gate, another toward a side door. Thinking I am walking in the wrong direction, I change
course and follow on the heels of the group walking toward the main entrance. Others do the same
until someone, probably Yvette, tells us to go toward "the door." We reverse direction and strag-
gle into the building through the correct entrance,
then up several flights of stairs, down a long hall-
way into the first and larger of two connecting
and almost empty rooms. The floors are the original 18th century wide planks and resound to our
steps with a hearty clatter. Adjacent to the larger
room is an even larger auditorium filled to capacity
with rows of chairs. Yvette tells me we will be able
to perform in the auditorium. I begin to imagine
the main performance taking place in there, with

sounds emanating from the rooms adjacent to it, which, as of this writing, I shall refer to as rooms #1 and #2.

But for the time being we shall work in rooms #1 and #2 and not in the chair-clotted auditorium. We clear some wooden slats from room #1 and put them in a storage area across the corridor. (Later when I have a fleeting urge to recover this material and repeat the action of "clearing" it, I find the storage room locked. By the time the caretaker unlocks this room several days later, I will have forgotten the original reason for my request.)

I suggest we enter room #1 from the auditorium and walk in the same patterns as we did in the courtyard. After doing that, I ask them to run in the same patterns. Following this, we pause near the doorway to room #2. I say, "Why don't we try doing the same thing in the other room?" We run into room #2 and execute the same patterns. I ask them to go back to room #1 and re-create the dialogue that had taken place just before the last maneuver, to be preceded by my "Why don't we . . ." (Marie asks Maria from Malmö what group she was in. Maria from Malmö replies something like "I was going toward the toilet." Marie says "Then you should be with us." Maria accordingly moves over. We all then run into room #2.)

Siemi performs her presentation, which she had prepared prior to my arrival, a combination of moving and speaking. It is very polished. Her experience and professionalism are very apparent and dominate my impression. We talk about that for a bit. I am concerned already about how to integrate different levels of performing experience into a whole. (Yvette, as it turns out, is especially concerned about this with regard to Siemi.) In the afternoon Siemi performs the sequence of gestures she had observed in the morning. Her style is percussive and dance-like, not at all like everyday gestures. I ask her to soften her movement. She says "sloppy" and repeats the sequence. I express approval and ask, "Did that feel sloppy?" She says "No." I am aware of imposing my bias, but feel justified, given the time constraint of four and a half days in which to come up with something I can call a "performance." If Siemi's style sets the standard, the others will be at a disadvantage. Easier (and far preferable from my point of view) to expand Siemi's horizons than to drill the others in some kind of dancerly performance mode.

I give a rudimentary explanation of my interest in "ordinary" movement, how people are not accustomed to thinking about it as performance, how our expectations as audience are usually geared toward some kind of transformation, how potential performers such as themselves can begin to see their untrained physicality as a resource. I stress the importance for someone of Siemi's experience to challenge and expand her habitual ways of doing things.

Karena presents her "staring piece." It begins with Rega seated behind a table staring at five others facing her in a row about four feet from the table. After several minutes four leave and place their chairs on either side of Rega. There are now five people behind the table staring at Maria from Malmö, who has remained in place. The first loner can be seen as some kind of authority figure or judge appraising a group of supplicants. The second solitary figure becomes a criminal being judged by a jury. The relation of chairs to table is the deciding factor.

Elsebeth has brought in string and instruction books for the whole group with which to play Cat's

Cradle. We all pair off and try to do it. I suggest Elsebeth play it with Marie, who has the assignment of describing a "walk in the city." The two activities can occur simultaneously.

I notice that Orse, an extremely shy Hungarian woman who speaks and understands hardly any English, has taken her assignment very seriously and has been moving around the room in slow motion regardless of what the others are doing. I start laughing and have to admit that I had entirely forgotten that I had given her that slip of paper.

I try to stage all of the assignments that have been carried out. Anders's contribution is to sit cross-legged on the floor, drawing in a self-absorbed way on a pad of paper. He has already shown signs of discontent. What is taking place here is apparently not what he expected. Nevertheless, I stow his activity in my mental archive as something potentially useful.

As we are ending the session, I catch Jens and Anders doing some pugilistic fooling around and suggest that the two of them work out the assignment of "Emotional Gestures" (which will eventually become "Romantic Trio").

Yvette, Amy, and I again have dinner together. When I get back to the hotel I notice that my clothes reek from the day's and evening's accumulation of smoke. I must stifle my horror that all of my students, most of them in their early twenties, are avid smokers.

Tuesday

I learn from the concierge that the auditorium is barred to us because of the fragility of the mural on the ceiling of the room below. I resign myself to working and performing in the two smaller spaces. I report this to the group. Michelle suggests that, weather permitting, we could do the performance outside. I immediately veto that suggestion without explaining why. A reflex dictated by the lack of time to transpose material from one space to a totally different one. We have fewer than five days. (It doesn't occur to me until Michelle reminds me two days later over drinks that my response was discomfitingly abrupt.)

Arthur shows up for the first time. I give him the assignment of defining "happening." Siemi informs me that due to a prior commitment she may not be able to be present on Friday, the day of the performance, but she would like to attend until then. I ask her to teach everyone her sequence of gestures, also to add to it. We all stand in a circle and practice and add to the sequence of pedestrian moves. One of them is a habitual gesture of Yvette's, who happens to be present while we are working on this exercise. She enters the process with good natured humor, allowing the group to appropriate this token of her hitherto unselfconscious dailiness.

Clasp hands behind head.
Do "Yvette's" parallel forearms to right.
Look over left shoulder, look straight ahead.
Lean hands on knees, look right, then left.
Straighten up while right hand wipes mouth with sniff.
Brush dust off thighs.
Scratch neck with left hand.
Brush hair back with right hand.
Exhale with a loud "Ha!"
Lift right hip and leg to side.
Shake left hand at arm's length beside thigh.

Marie contributes a card game involving four people. I file this away as a suitable event to follow the running. The concentration demanded by the task immediately eliminates the possibility of self-consciousness.

We look at various people's execution of their assignments.

Anders seems to have dropped out. I assign the "Emotional Gestures" to Jens and Karena. There is much hilarity as they work up the sequence while the rest of us watch.

I add further assignments:

> Bring in a text dealing with sex, race, or class. Think about ways of presenting it not only as a straight reading.
> Bring in an object and devise a group activity around it. Think about sound or music that can accompany the activities.

Wednesday

People show their objects. We are all nonplussed by Karena's plaster bell pepper and red feather boa, Jen's passport, a fetish-like thing wrapped in blue plastic twine, some seashells, a brick. Arthur's black rubber-wrapped megaphone is the only object that suggests immediate use. He will speak his rap about happenings through it.

Long-haired Maria announces she would prefer to be a spectator rather than a performer. I ask her why. She is unclear about her reason. I don't argue, and she sits on the sidelines.

I have decided that the audience will at first be stationed in room #1 and the opening maneuver of the "Vaudeville" will be the surging of the whole group into room #1 from room #2, followed by the pause and regrouping with discussion before running back into room #2. The activities that will follow the running and be performed simultaneously in room #1 have begun to accumulate:

1) The card players; 2) Orse walks and gestures in slow motion; 3) Rega walks back and forth talking about modern dance; 4) Maria from Malmö does various things with a chair and string; 5) Marie describes a walk in the city while doing Cat's Cradle with Elsebeth; 6) Arthur talks about happenings.

It is a miniature Tower of Babel!

The card game involves feats of memory. About three dozen cards with photos of Japanese cuisine on one side are spread face down in a grid pattern. Each player has two turns turning over cards. The object is to remember the exact placement of a given card and try to match it with its double. The players had been Jens, Michelle, Rega, and long-haired Maria, but now Maria has dropped out. As we are discussing whether to do it with three people or appoint a fourth, long-haired Maria changes her mind and says she will participate. I give her an ultimatum: "You're either in or out. Make up your mind." She says she has been "silly," that there's no good reason for her to be a spectator. I don't say it, but I hope she has a better reason to be a participant.

I am entranced by Orse's dreamy walking. She ever so slowly brings her hands to her face and down again as she walks. Maria from Malmö rolls her chair around, ties it to a pipe, talks softly to it, strokes it as though it is a pet.

Arthur contributes a CD of a black rap group that he wants to try out with the card game. We play it and are startled at the contrast between the ghetto lyrics and the blond Nordic card players. He thinks—and I agree—the two should go together.

Karena reports she would like to try out an audio tape of a cat purring to accompany her Staring Piece. The trouble is it's on a DAT, and Michelle's recorder, which we have been using, plays only CDs or regular cassettes. Michelle offers to transfer the DAT to a cassette.

Marie, Karena, Michelle, and Rega have brought texts, seemingly without a clue as to how to stage them. Rega reads from Henry Miller. I suggest she climb up and down a tall ladder that had been left in room #2. It is a very lovely performance. Looking like a tiny sprite, she hikes up her long skirt and carefully picks her way up and over the top and down the other side while reading in a delicate wavering voice. Somehow Elsebeth gets into an argument with her. Elsebeth hates Henry Miller, while Rega loves the writing. I ask if they can conduct the argument while climbing up and down the ladder. They at first balk, feel that their arguing is too private an activity. Finally they agree on Rega reading and when she pauses Elsebeth will intervene with several sentences, like "Henry Miller makes me feel like a victim."

In Danish, Karena reads something by a newspaper columnist that is somewhat anti-feminist. When she has roughly translated it for my benefit and indicated its bias, I ask "What can you do to show that you don't agree with him?" Marie and Maria from Malmö then work out a succession of moves that consists of toppling Karena over in her chair and manipulating her body as she continues to read, finally walking her into a wall and leaving her there.

We discuss what language the performance

should be conducted in. Two of the texts brought in are in English; others are Danish newspaper clippings. It seems best not to translate the original language of each text, and whatever other speech takes place should be in Danish, or, if I am involved, in English.

Marie has devised some simple moves to accompany her reading of a news report about immigrants and unemployment. It is a concise and economical performance, taking her in four stages from sitting on the floor to sitting in a chair and underscoring different parts of her text.

I teach several of my standard configurations: "L'Informe" and "Clump." I insert Michelle's reading (in English) of a sociological text about Danish identity into the Clump.

In the afternoon we meet in the media room, where Jens and Rega show videotapes. Rega's tape is a loop of jump-cuts of Elizabeth Taylor's "breathing moments" in *Who's Afraid of Virginia Woolf?* I ask her what she would like to do with the tape— wheel it around as it plays on a monitor, for instance? She says what she's really interested in is the inhalations. I suggest we as a group do them in quick succession. The exercise proves very effective: the intake of breath moves from one to another, then in the next round is exhaled, to be inhaled once more, etc. Someone suggests we do it as a "clump." It breaks us all up. Somehow, the initial tension in the group is broken in this ridiculously forced physical proximity with one another while breathing. We return to the original sequential breathing while sitting and standing around the table. Long-haired Maria suggests reading her text, a list of women astronomers, after several rounds of breathing and while the group breathing continues. We all agree this is a successful combination of sound and image.

Jens's tape shows him in front of a building bellowing behind a mask "I am alone. Who is there?" . . . etc. and somersaulting down a hill. I ask him if he knows of Samuel Beckett. He doesn't. I explain why I've made this association and suggest he perform the mask part of the video in the first section in room #1.

Thursday

Andrea shows up for the first time. She has just returned from New York. I am at first doubtful that she can be integrated into the piece at this late date. She is game for whatever she can pick up and begins by learning Siemi's gesture sequence, which we again practice.

Marie reports that after talking it over at lunch the previous day, they thought it might be a good idea to just choose the activities freely in performance. I gulp and resist my impulse to "just say no." I explain that it is a matter of expediency to predetermine the order of the program. It would take much longer than the time available to us to work out all the possibilities of transition between group and individual activities if we were to use "spontaneous determination" in the performance itself. Without working out the details beforehand, their "freedom" might result in a mess. Better to know what we are doing. To handle things like freedom and indeterminacy well requires experience and time. What I don't say is that I'm the one with the most experience here and that they should trust me. There is a certain paradox here that will emerge the next day.

Karena tries out her Staring Piece with the "purring" tape Michelle has transferred. It is an odd combination, both sound and image singularly charged. Karena is pleased. I think it's a hit. I seem to remember I said as much.

I teach "Line with objects." The incongruous collection now finds its place. The brick, bell pepper, newspaper, book, and a feather from Karena's boa are the objects ultimately used, passed from hand to hand as the line continually reconfigures itself. A problem arises: where to keep the objects before they are needed? After much debate (and a bit of mock frustrated groaning on my part) Michelle suggests they be put in a basket which I will carry and from which I will distribute them during "L'Informe."

We start to run through the entire sequence of events, which I had tentatively organized the previous night. Afterwards there are suggestions for changes. Jens doesn't feel right about his mask bit, and others remark that it doesn't fit, that it's too sentimental for this context. I am pleased that by this point there is a consensus about "fitness." They have a good sense of where the piece seems to be heading. I suggest he read his text—a news clipping about Bill Gates—while holding the mask to his face. But his mask is opaque. What to do? Michelle again comes to the rescue. She will bring a transparent plastic bowl that can serve as a mask and through which Jens will be able to read the clipping.

Arthur is tired of talking about happenings. "Could I sing a song?" He ends up singing "La Paloma" in German out of the open window through his megaphone. He is very striking in an S&M way with his jet-black hair, black shirt, and black leather pants. (I learn he is Austrian, a sword swallower, and does "vomit performances" with a partner.)

I suggest that Jens and Arthur do a gay version of "Emotional Gestures." Again there is much hilarity as they work. There follows a discussion about how to integrate the two versions, the gay and the straight. Various strategies are tried. Finally someone suggests that Jens remain in the middle and after completing the sequence with Arthur, he should turn to Karena and do it with her. This version is approved by all. And slow sleepy Jens is pleased because the strain of doing most of it on one knee (to which he descends to express the initial "I love you") will be shared by both knees. They will keep repeating the sequence until the group doing "L'Informe" moves from room #2 into room #1.

I add a Dada bit for the opening collage in room #1: Karena and I walk toward each other on the diagonal. YR: "Where is the post office?" Karena: "What's that to me?" I exit through the door, and Karena goes to the corner.

We work on the logistics of transitions. Yvette is the guardian of the tape recorder, which will have to be moved from room #1 to room #2. In room #1 Yvette will turn it on and off. In room #2, Karena will take care of it.

Friday

Amy and her painting students arrive with nine painted balls they have been working on for the last week. Yvette will roll them into either of the two rooms at irregularly spaced intervals throughout the performance. The performers and audience will simply have to move them aside or keep out of their way. There is some discussion as to how fragile the balls are. They are large balloons that had first been covered in papier mâché, then painted in decorative and figurative patterns. In transit to our part of the building, some of them seem to have deflated a bit.

Orse and Andrea have not shown up. Yvette asks me if I'm nervous. I reply that I'm not nervous, I'm pissed off.

We start to rehearse without them. Arthur thinks that the two readings by Karena and Marie should be broken up by something else. I teach him a Futurist bit: Man enters room in an overcoat . . . Jens lends Arthur his overcoat, and after several forays in which he breaks up laughing, Arthur does a superb agitated entrance looking at the passport he has found in the pocket, then goes to a window, turns, sees the audience, shouts "I have no idea why I'm here!" and leaves. Jens and Karena will then follow him out to begin "Emotional Gestures" ("Romantic Trio") in room #1.

There are still glitches in the transitions. I ask them if they want another rehearsal. They are unanimous. We agree to break for lunch and reconvene at 1:00 and be through in time for the 3 PM performance.

After lunch, everyone assembles on time, including Orse and Andrea. (Orse had problems with her young daughter that morning; the child had smeared her face with colored inks from laundry markers just before leaving for day-care.) All the kinks are worked out. At one point in my somewhat autocratic efforts to marshal the attention of the group, Arthur reminds me—in an affectionate manner—of the preliminary email I had sent to them before arriving, in which I exhorted them to "keep in mind the value of mistakes, failures, interruptions, breakdowns, interferences, accidents, incompletions, muddles, mix-ups . . . and chance occurrences." There is no time to do anything but laugh.

Later, however, I think of what I could have said: that this statement refers to the *process* of making something, not only to its realization. There was the "accident" of the courtyard "muddle" and "mix-up"; the "interferences" of the simultaneous talking; the "chance occurrence" of the way the balls entered the spaces; the "interruption" of the Dada encounter; the "mistakes" engendered by having to read a text while doing "Clump," etc., etc.

Amy arrives and is jubilant that the balls have regained their original fullness. Everyone is alert and excited. I relax. An overflow crowd begins to gather in room #1. At 3:15 PM we begin. The performance lasts about a half hour and everything goes smoothly.

Afterward

Email correspondence with Steve Paxton[3]
    April 25, 2000
    Dear Yvonne:
    . . . In your journal you definitely passed with flying colors that always awkward moment with a group when they start wanting to resort to anarchy and improvisation, to slip the traces which they have paid to import. It is a bit different from

---

3. Steve Paxton was a dancer and choreographer, a founding member of Judson Dance Theater, and a frequent collaborator with Yvonne Rainer.

CPAD, I think, in that we took a year's transition, but it is of a sort.[4]

As you retained the reins in this event, what is your assessment of it? It sounds to me like you managed to collect much of the extrania in the process into the show, nimble and focused.

And, what is the physical posture for "I am gay"?

[Steve Paxton]

April 25, 2000

Dear Steve:

Yes, it's a very precarious line I tread when I go into these situations and know but don't fully reveal to them, at least at the beginning, the degree to which I shall be holding the reins. In the two previous situations—NYU and Chicago—because of more extended time, I gave them a lot more to work with, like all kinds of films and readings from which they extrapolated performance ideas. But in Denmark I had them read, prior to my arrival, several essays on my own work [by Peggy Phelan and Noel Carroll], and when I got there, I showed several of my films and did my standard lecture "Out of a Corner of the 60s," which encompasses a smattering of Cage, Cunningham, and happenings, but is mainly about Judson. All as introduction to certain ideas. Then it was like pulling teeth or rabbits out of a hat or ideas out of a kind of Y.R. geist. They were finally very appreciative and exhilarated, as was much of the audience response, and there were no real rebellions. Probably

---

4. *Continuous Project-Altered Daily,* a dance work by Rainer from 1969–70, which eventually morphed into the improvisation-based group *Grand Union.*

because once the ball got rolling it was very clear that I was open to concrete suggestions and not to vague fantasies of "freedom."

To express "I am gay," Jens, a large sleepy, slow student who did much of the exercise on one knee (to which he initially repaired to express "I love you") simply turned his head from his "Why did you leave me?" posture and looked at his partner. Nothing special, but effective nonetheless.

Email correspondence with Gregg Bordowitz[5]

April 27, 2000

Dear Why,

. . . One of the most exciting things about your teaching process is the way you incorporate material generated from the classroom experience immediately into the developing "text" of the class. I love reading how the performances unfold out of each other, kind of like a complicated origami figure unfolded, then refolded into something even more wonderfully complex.

. . . Finally, I would love to read your thoughts on why pedestrian, everyday movement is more compelling to you than the studied, refined and/or confident movements of dancers and performers. This has been an important issue for you throughout your career. It's an important part of your filmmaking. Why does it remain so? How has your thinking on this changed over the years? Has it changed? Why do teaching situations bring up the issue of everyday movement for you with fresh intensity?

[Gregg Bordowitz]

---

5. Gregg Bordowitz is a writer and artist.

Biographies

Yvonne Rainer, one of the founders of the Judson Dance Theater, made a transition to filmmaking following a fifteen-year career as a choreographer/dancer (1960–75). After making seven experimental feature-length films, she returned to dance in 2000 via a commission from the Baryshnikov Dance Foundation (*After Many a Summer Dies the Swan*). Her dances and films have been seen throughout the United States, Europe, and Asia in concert halls and museum retrospectives. Her publications include *Feelings Are Facts: A Life; Work: 1961–73; The Films of Yvonne Rainer; A Woman Who . . . : Essays, Interviews, Scripts; Moving and Being Moved;* and *Revisions.* Her awards include two Guggenheim Fellowships, a MacArthur Fellowship, a U.S.A. Fellowship, and a Yoko Ono Courage Award.

Emmanuèle Phuon has performed internationally with the Elisa Monte Dance Company, Martha Clarke, Baryshnikov's White Oak Dance Project, and Yvonne Rainer. Her choreographic work has been commissioned and presented at the Baryshnikov Arts Center, New Haven's International Festival of Arts and Ideas, the Spoleto Festival in Charleston, S.C., the Guggenheim Museum's Works and Process, the Singapore da:ns festival, Danspace Project in New York, and more. Among them,

Khmeropedies III / Source: Primate earned the support and endorsement of His Majesty King Sihamoni. Ms. Phuon is currently on the faculty at Montclair State University, Yale University, and NYU Tisch School of Arts. She has contributed a chapter on postmodern dance to *Milestones in Dance in the USA* (2022) and is the author of an issue of *Dance Index* (Winter 2022–23).

Pascal Lemaître is a freelance author and illustrator based in Belgium. His editorial work has appeared in the *New Yorker,* the *New York Times, Le Monde, Liberation, Le 1, Astrapi,* and *J'aime Lire,* among other publications. His illustrations for children's and adult books can be found in the catalogues of many American, Belgian, and French publishers such as L'école des loisirs/Collection Pastel, Éditions de l'Aube, Simon & Schuster, Scholastic, and Penguin Books. Pascal has had the enormous privilege of working with authors Toni and Slade Morrison, Stéphane Hessel, Edgar Morin, Boris Cyrulnik, Jean-Claude Ameisen, Pierre Rahbi, and Rascal. *Come with Me,* by Holly M. McGhee, illustrated by Pascal, is a *New York Times* best seller. In 2015, the Museum Tomi Ungerer curated an exhibit titled *Tomi Ungerer Invites Pascal Lemaître,* featuring Pascal's illustrations for children's books. Among them, *The Book of Mean People* by Toni and Slade Morrison prompted legendary illustrator and author Bill Steig to exclaim, "These drawings are wonderful, and you can quote me!"